JOB: WHERE IS GOD IN MY SUFFERING?

Marc Davis

STUDY GUIDE WITH LEADER'S NOTES

New Growth Press
newgrowthpress.com

For Susan, who said I should write.

The content of this book is based on a sermon series I preached at City Line Church in Bala Cynwyd, Pennsylvania. They were gracious and encouraging, and I am grateful.

New Growth Press, Greensboro, NC 27401
newgrowthpress.com

Cover Design: Faceout Books, faceoutstudio.com
Interior Typesetting and eBook: Lisa Parnell, lparnellbookservices.com
Exercises and Application Questions: Jack Klumpenhower

ISBN 978-1-64507-421-2 (paperback)
ISBN 978-1-64507-422-9 (ebook)

Printed in India

29 28 27 26 25   2 3 4 5 6

CONTENTS

OUTLINE OF THE BOOK OF JOB

Chapters 1–2	The front bookend: what happened to Job
Chapter 3	Job's lament
Chapters 4–27	Cycles of discourse: Job's debate with Eliphaz, Bildad, and Zophar
Chapter 28	A poem on wisdom and where to find it
Chapters 29–31	Job's final words
Chapters 32–37	Elihu's reply
Chapters 38–41	The Lord speaks
Chapter 42	The back bookend: what happened afterward

INTRODUCTION

The book of Job is not an easy read for twenty-first-century Western people. Its opening and closing chapters feel disturbing to many of us. The bulk of the book is a cycle of dialogues that seem to lead nowhere productive. And God's answer to Job at the end of the book can seem to be no answer at all. Easier to skip this part of your Bible reading plan! But the rewards of studying Job come to those who are willing to give it a slow read, to camp out in its questions and talk to God about the issues it raises, to engage relationally with him within the spaces the book creates for such conversations.

One of the things Job clearly teaches is to resist the impulse to give simplistic answers to human anguish. Such answers are a way of keeping the lived experience of suffering at arm's length. Job's suffering is uncomfortable for us because it raises the specter of suffering that might hit closer to home. As with Job's friends, so for us: "You see something dreadful and are afraid" (6:21 NIV). But neither avoiding the issues nor pat theological answers will stave off the seriousness of the things we have to think about.

The way through the *something dreadful* is to reflect on Job's story, and your own story, in light of Jesus's story. Job the innocent sufferer points to Jesus, the ultimate innocent sufferer. Jesus, too, endured horrible suffering, both physical and spiritual, that at the time seemed absolutely meaningless and unfruitful. But more was going on than met the eye—as Job said, "Things too wonderful for me, which I did not know" (42:3). As with the other resources in this series, you will study Job with that wonderful story of Jesus in mind.

HOW TO USE THIS STUDY

This study guide is designed to help you learn from Job within a small group. Job is written in the form of a dialogue between friends. Its wisdom is not in quick answers, but in the process of taking turns, listening to others, and speaking from the heart about hard things. The participants in Job grieve, get frustrated, struggle to understand, and sometimes just want to be silent for a while. Try to make your group a place where people feel free to do the same.

Each participant should have one of these study guides in order to join in reading and be able to work through the exercises during that part of the study. The study leader should read through both the lesson and the leader's notes in the back of this book before each lesson begins. No other preparation or homework is required.

There are eight lessons in this study guide. Each will take about an hour to complete, perhaps a bit more if your group is large, and will include these elements:

BIG IDEA. This is a summary of the main point of the lesson.

BIBLE CONVERSATION. You will read a passage from Job and discuss it. As the heading suggests, the Bible conversation questions are intended to spark a conversation rather than generate correct answers. The leader's notes at the back of this book provide some insights, but don't just turn there for the "right answer." At times you may want to see what the notes say, but always try to answer for yourself first by thinking about the Bible passage.

ARTICLE. This is the main teaching section of the lesson, written by the book's author.

DISCUSSION. The discussion questions following the article will help you apply the teaching to your life.

EXERCISE. The exercise is a section you will complete on your own during group time. You can write in the book if that helps you. You will then share some of what you learned with the group. If the group is large, it may help to split up to share the results of the exercise and to pray, so that everyone has a better opportunity to participate.

WRAP-UP AND PRAYER. God is a part of your conversation. He will speak to you through the Bible, and you will speak to him in prayer. Make this a much-anticipated element of the group dialogue.

Jesus's suffering turned out not to be evidence of God's harshness, capriciousness, or indifference to people, but instead the ultimate evidence of God's determination to redeem. As you embark on this study, keep his story in view. That story is the one that makes sense of your own.

Lesson

1

MEET THE INNOCENT SUFFERER

BIG IDEA

Your relationship with God through Jesus is not a predictable "business" relationship, but a more complicated—and better—friendship founded on grace.

BIBLE CONVERSATION *20 MINUTES*

For Job's original Jewish audience, the story arc of the book would have been familiar. It was an old story, set in antiquity outside of Israel, and Israel's Gentile neighbors had their own versions of the tale. Everyone knew the basic gist: Job was a good man who nevertheless suffered in awful ways.

The first two chapters of Job, together with most of the last chapter, provide a narrative frame for the poetic heart of the book. These bookends establish the context for the agonizing struggle of the chapters in between.

When someone tells you their own story of suffering, they aren't usually looking for advice or interpretation. They're just trusting you with their story and inviting you to hold it with them. Think of the introduction to Job in much the same way. Now have someone read **Job chapter 1** aloud, or have a few readers take turns. Then discuss the questions below:

What do you find most interesting or impressive about the person of Job before his calamity? Explain.

How do you respond emotionally to this chapter, or what hard questions do you want answered going forward?

Look at what comes from Job's heart and mouth in verses 21 and 22. How might you reword his speech to fit our present time or your way of speaking?

****

Next, read this lesson's article. Take turns reading it aloud, switching readers at each paragraph break. Then discuss the questions that follow.

Lesson 1

ARTICLE

THE TERMS OF THE RELATIONSHIP

5 MINUTES

I've been taking our cars to the same mechanic for twenty-five years. Jim knows my name; I ask after his family. He does his work well, and over the years he's made a little money off our aging vehicles.

I like Jim. But my relationship with him is essentially a transactional relationship. It works on this principle: when I have a problem with my car, I give Jim money and he makes the problem go away. You do this, I'll do that, everyone's happy. But if I become unhappy with his work, there's nothing to keep me from saying, "There are other mechanics. Maybe I'll go somewhere else."

The book of Job is an extended conversation about the terms of a person's relationship with God. What do I need to understand in order to make this relationship work? Is it like my relationship with Jim the mechanic? *God, I'll do this, you do that, everyone's happy.* Is there a pattern to rely on, that if I do ABC, good things will happen to me, but if I do XYZ, bad things will happen? It's not an intellectual discussion. It's a gut-level struggle to find some workable place to plant your flag and live your life.

There are two things to know about Job. First, Job was "blameless and upright, one who feared God and turned away from evil" (v. 1). The narrator wants us to get this straight up front, because later in the book people will question whether that is really true. But here it is: Job was a good man.

What's the second thing to know about Job? Verse 2, lots of children. Verse 3, lots of animals and "very many servants." By all measures in his culture, Job was a rich, blessed man. So he was a good man and he was a rich man. He did things right, and things went well for him.

Hmm, both good and rich! Is there a cause and effect there? Is Job rich *because* he is good? And if so, is that his reason for doing good? Chapter 1 records a heavenly conversation that Job is not privy to. Satan tells God that Job is only in it for the blessing. His "godliness" is transactional, nothing more. If you take away the blessing, Job's good life will evaporate.

What follows is not just a downturn in circumstances but a tsunami of suffering. Job loses everything. His neighbors observe it and try to make sense of it. It's perplexing, because everyone had understood Job's prosperity as evidence of God's favor on his life. And by the normal standard of Old Testament wisdom, they weren't wrong.

According to many Bible verses, if you want a happy and blessed life, what should you do? The broad-brushstrokes right answer is: fear God, do what's right, and it will tend to work out for you. But that's not one-size-fits-all wisdom. It doesn't explain everything, everywhere, all the time.

Job's neighbors observe the disaster in his life and they apply that broad-brushstrokes principle in reverse. Job is experiencing bad outcomes, so he must have done something to make God angry. The book of Job doesn't reject the idea that Job's prosperity was an expression of God's blessing. But is suffering then evidence of God's displeasure? The people assume it must be. *Job, what did you do?*

But there was no scandal, no double life. Job's testimony is that he's suffering but is innocent of any serious outward sin, and he is telling the truth. This is a new idea. Nobody in Job's community has a category for this. So for the next thirty-five chapters, people will tell him he's lying: Are you saying God isn't fair? Who do you think you are? The innocent sufferer? That man doesn't exist. And Job says, you just met him.

What if I told you that embedded in this story is the seed of something very, very good—a better kind of relationship with God? Better than a business relationship. Better than a reliable transactional agreement. Transactional religion is me-centered: my goal is to achieve XYZ, and I enlist God to help me get there. *Lord, there is a script for us both to follow, you as well as me.* But he is not interested in that plan.

The journey Jesus takes you on is better, and the pattern of the innocent sufferer is central to it. The ultimate innocent sufferer, Jesus, is the pivotal character of human history. By his life, suffering, death, and resurrection, Jesus changes the principle that governs human relationships with God. Instead of *you get what you deserve*, the new governing principle is grace. And the person who knows Jesus by grace is invited into so much more than a life in which things go predictably right.

In John 15:15 Jesus says, "No longer do I call you servants, for the servant does not know what his master is doing; but I have called you friends, for all that I have heard from my Father I have made known to you." Jesus lets his friends in on the mystery of the cross. He tells them, "The Son of Man must suffer many things" (Luke 9:22), and at first they recoil from it: *What are you saying? Stop talking like that!* But this is the way of healing and restoration.

The suffering of Jesus will spill over into the lives of his friends, not just to Peter and John, but also to you and me. "We always carry around in our body the death of Jesus, so that the life of Jesus may also be revealed in our body" (2 Corinthians 4:10 NIV). In a mysterious way, it's a sharing with Jesus in the big plan to make all things new.

Job 1 ends with worship. It's a simple expression of a mature relationship that is more than paying the bill to God for services rendered. God is calling us into a similar relationship of trust and love. That doesn't mean that the road ahead won't at times be agonizing, and the fleshing out of this relationship hard work. But our ability to, like Job, engage relationally with God in all kinds of circumstances sets us on a course for stability in an unpredictable world.

DISCUSSION *10 MINUTES*

The article says it's better to share in Jesus's life than to have a life that goes predictably right. Are you quick to agree, or is it hard for you to accept that? Explain.

How is Job's story, and Jesus's story, similar to your own life story so far?

Lesson 1

EXERCISE

TRANSACTIONAL THINKING

20 MINUTES

Even if you know better, at times you might still treat your life with God as a transactional relationship. You act, feel, or secretly suspect you must conduct business with God rather than receive grace from him. Signs of this might include:

- You sense God will reward you with a pleasant life if you do ____________________.
- You worry God will trouble you if you disobey or don't ____________________.
- You feel you shouldn't have to ____________________ for God unless he seems to be blessing you.
- You sense you might give up doing ____________________ for God if it doesn't seem to be "working" for you, or if God stops showing he appreciates your efforts.
- You realize you would be glad if God's command to ____________________ did not exist so that you would not have to deal with it.

For this exercise, you will work on your own to fill in some similar blanks. Work through both parts of the exercise below. When the group is ready, you will share and discuss some of your responses.

PART 1: Being transactional with God. Each prompt below describes an area of the Christian life. Despite these things being good, you might sometimes think about them in transactional terms—that you and God trade obedience for blessings. Read each description. For some of them, give a specific example that fits you. You do not need to fill in every blank, just those where you have something to share.

A godly behavior. Some way you might practice care for others, purity, generosity, truth-telling, or other moral conduct God has commanded.

I get transactional about being ______________________ for God.

A spiritual discipline. Some way you might be diligent in prayer, churchgoing, Bible reading, family devotions, fasting, etc.

I get transactional about doing ______________________ for God.

Christian service. Some kind of church or mission work, godly cause, aid for others, witness about Jesus, etc.

I get transactional about doing ______________________ for God.

Progress against sin in your life. Some habit of unkindness, impurity, greed, dishonesty, or other wrongdoing to overcome.

I get transactional about how much I resist

____.

An emotional experience. Some joy, godly sorrow, passion in worship, sense of nearness/honesty with God, feeling of sincerity in your life with God, etc.

I get transactional about feeling

____.

An approval standard. Some church/theological affiliation, political stance, success of family/children, standing in work or school, physical appearance, or other marker that says you are the right kind of person.

I get transactional about having a right

____.

PART 2: Sharing Jesus's death and life. Instead of a transactional relationship with God, the gospel gives you a much richer bond. By faith you are joined to Jesus and to his whole life story. In 2 Corinthians, the apostle Paul tells how his missionary work for God did not bring a pleasant life in return, but instead came with suffering. Paul sees this as a precious wonder: he is so joined to Jesus that he both suffers with Jesus and shares Jesus's glories. Read what Paul writes about it below. Note a few aspects of being joined to Jesus (you might circle or underline them) that you find especially meaningful.

> He who raised the Lord Jesus will raise us also with Jesus and bring us with you into his presence. For it is all for your sake, so that as grace extends to more and more people it may increase thanksgiving, to the glory of God.
>
> So we do not lose heart. Though our outer self is wasting away, our inner self is being renewed day by day. For this light momentary affliction is preparing for us an eternal weight of glory beyond all comparison. (2 Corinthians 4:14–17)

When the group is ready, share some of your responses. What are some ways you get transactional with God? Explain what you feel God expects of you and what you expect of him.

What did you note in the 2 Corinthians passage, and why is that part meaningful to you?

WRAP-UP AND PRAYER *10 MINUTES*

There are no easy answers to suffering and how it intertwines with God's blessings, his fatherly discipline, and our companionship with Jesus. Knowing this, make wrestling with God in prayer a part of your study of Job. Pray together, taking your concerns to God, and asking him to use this study for good in your lives.

Lesson

2

LAMENT FROM THE ASH HEAP

BIG IDEA

Job's lament gives us words for our own experience. As we speak our trouble, his experience and our experience and the experience of Jesus all converge in a companionship of suffering.

BIBLE CONVERSATION *20 MINUTES*

In Job chapter 2, the devastating losses of chapter 1 are made worse by the addition of painful sores all over Job's body. Here we get the unforgettable, pathetic image of Job sitting among the ashes, scraping his skin with a piece of broken pottery. Then we read about the arrival of three friends: Eliphaz, Bildad, and Zophar. They have heard about Job's troubles and have come together to sympathize with him and comfort him. They are appalled when they see him, and have the good sense at first just to be his companions in suffering: "They sat with him on the ground seven days and seven nights, and no one spoke a word to him, for they saw that his suffering was very great" (2:13).

Now in chapter 3 begins the heart of the book. It consists of cycles of back-and-forth between Job and the friends, whose "friendship" becomes increasingly unhelpful as the conversation continues. Job will speak first, uttering a curse against the day of his birth. He wishes he had never been born or had been stillborn.

Understand that in Job, not everything said is good or right. Job and his friends speak out of their limited human understanding, and out of their own hearts' interpretations of what they see, hear, and experience. Often their words are partly right or true in a sense, or they express something that feels basically right but still can be better tuned with further wisdom. At other times their words are just off target and unhelpful. With this in mind, have someone read **Job chapter 3** aloud, or have a few readers take turns. As you read, notice Job's logic and why he finds the idea of not having lived appealing. Then discuss the questions below:

What parts of Job's curse make you think, *I can understand why he thinks or feels that way*? Explain.

How does Job's state of mind affect you emotionally as you read about it?

In verse 10 Job expresses the longing that trouble would have been hidden from his eyes—that he would have never lived to experience what he experienced. What kind of trouble might make you feel something similar?

****

Now take turns reading the article aloud, switching readers for each paragraph. Then discuss the questions that follow.

Lesson

2

ARTICLE

SPEAK YOUR TROUBLE

5 MINUTES

When you have been in distress, have you ever said something that made people uncomfortable? And has anyone said back to you, "Please don't say that"? Or have you reacted that way yourself when someone else was in distress and said something raw and unsettling? Have you ever told them, "Don't say that"?

What can we do with our anguish? Does it have to be bottled? Must we be restrained at all times? If your thoughts go to extreme places, can those thoughts ever be spoken out loud for others to hear?

Mental health professionals often speak of grief and trauma as things that need to be metabolized. This means they need to be deeply processed, body and soul. There is a need for these life experiences to be digested, and part of that process is a need for trouble to be spoken. It must be put into words. But when the pain is acute, the speaking of that pain will very often seem extreme and shocking to other people.

In the Bible, speaking your trouble to God is called *lament* and it is what you do. It's what Job does. How can we sort out his lament? A good place to start may be at the end of chapter 3, verses 25 and 26.

> "What I feared has come upon me;
>   what I dreaded has happened to me.

> I have no peace, no quietness;
> I have no rest, but only turmoil." (NIV)

These verses express two burdens that press upon Job: the burden of *past experience* and the burden of *present experience.* Verse 25 gives language to the struggle to get your head around the very hard things that may have taken place in your life. Verse 26 gives language to the struggle to go on living in the present after those things have happened.

In verse 25 Job says, to his own amazement, something like this: "The worst things I could ever have imagined are exactly the things that have happened to me. What was just the stuff of nightmares, my worst-case scenarios—those things have actually played out in time and space in my life. They are no longer hypotheticals; they are real-life events. Terrible things happened to my children. Terrible things happened to many people who worked for me, whose names and faces I knew. A natural disaster happened. Violence happened. These things came to pass in my household."

For each of us who reads the book of Job, Job's laments lend language to the events of our own lives. We too are people that things have happened to, sometimes in some sort of cause-and-effect relationship to our own decisions, but often not. You may have suffered an injury, maybe been disabled in a life-altering way. Some of us have been the victims of a crime, perhaps been robbed or assaulted. You've lost loved ones, perhaps suddenly. Some have lost a child. Maybe you've been ill treated by someone you trusted. You've been through a divorce. And these events may have been recent or they may have happened some years ago.

The text gives us a place to name these things, to count them before God. Even things that are not level-one losses need to be processed: the loss of a job, the loss of a friendship, the loss of a church home. These too are things to be spoken and grieved. In Isaiah 53:3 the

Messiah, the Lord Jesus, is said to be familiar with suffering. He has seen it. He has experienced it. He has known it from the inside. It's the same with Job.

There's an old African-American spiritual you may have heard. It would have been sung by people living in bondage, who had endured whippings and sexual assaults, and had seen their family members sold out of their lives forever. The song says, "Nobody knows the trouble I've seen." It's just that simple and just that devastating: These things happened. I've seen them. I've lived them. I was not spared from this experience. And it is tremendously weighty and isolating to live with what I've seen.

If you have suffered, this passage says you are not alone in that experience. And if your life has been a relatively easy one, it tells you to understand with kindness the weight that people bear, and have a heart of mercy.

The second part of the lament is, *what is life like now?* And again, Job speaks it: "I have no peace, no quietness." He is always agitated. He is always in turmoil. He cannot rest. His post-traumatic anxiety and depression are acute and chronic. In a word, Job's experience is "misery" (v. 20). If a friend said these things, it would tear your heart out. But if you can relate at all to Job's experience, maybe a text like this one can be a gift.

Throughout the book Job is desperately lonely and looking for someone to understand his experience. But in his loneliness, he himself becomes that understanding person for us. He becomes a companion who can understand our experiences. He's down in the dirt with us. And that is an extraordinary thing to find in your Bible.

Companionship is not efficient. It doesn't offer a fix. It says, "Let's sit together and hear each other out, uncensored, and see where that gets us."

But Job is not the only companion the Bible gives for people who suffer. There is a better companion for the person whose life does not make sense. That companion is the Lord Jesus. Jesus, unlike Job, is alive now. Where Job is a friend for you only in a literary sense, Jesus is present today with his people. Jesus, on the other side of his suffering, is attentive, interested, and available. And he says to you, "Come to me, all who labor and are heavy laden, and I will give you rest" (Matthew 11:28). He ministers to those who speak their trouble to him.

DISCUSSION *10 MINUTES*

In what way do you find it helpful—sometimes even necessary—to "speak your trouble"?

When has suffering made you feel isolated or lonely? How much did you know Jesus to be your companion at that time?

Lesson 2

EXERCISE

WHAT'S YOUR LAMENT?

20 MINUTES

A lament spoken to God is an exercise of faith. You tell about your hurts, believing that God listens and cares, and trusting that your companion Jesus is Lord over suffering and will never leave you.

For this exercise, you will work on your own to compose a short, personal lament that you will tell to God. Your lament might be about any sad or worrisome part of your life: family, work, relationships, health, etc. Laments in the Bible are often emotionally raw, so try to be open about hard feelings like:

Grief or sense of loss
Anxiety (about yourself or those you love)
Anger
Remorse
Shame

Follow the instructions below. When you finish, you won't be asked to share your lament with the group unless you want to, but you will have an opportunity to discuss the process of lamenting.

Compose your lament. Write a few lines of personal lament. Like Job who spoke in poetry, think of some words that sharply describe your experience or feelings. Fit those words into your lament. It might help to write out your lines of lament below:

____

____

____

____

____

____

Pray your lament. Now spend time with God in personal, silent prayer. Take the words you wrote and tell them to your Father, knowing that he hears and cares. Remember that Jesus, your companion in suffering, is alive and is also praying with you.

When the group is ready, discuss your time of lament. How did it feel to write and pray?

How might more lament be good for you, either individually or as a group?

WRAP-UP AND PRAYER *10 MINUTES*

Finish with group prayer. You might include some laments from the exercise if any of those were shared with the group.

Lesson

3

A DAY IN COURT

BIG IDEA

Jesus gives us the ability to enter into an otherwise-impossible, life-long dialogue with God.

BIBLE CONVERSATION *20 MINUTES*

Chapter 9 is Job's response to the counsel of his friend Bildad the Shuhite. Job's friend Eliphaz has spoken first, followed by Bildad, and both have assumed Job is suffering because he sinned. Nevertheless, Bildad has assured Job that he'll be restored if he repents: "If you will seek God and plead with the Almighty for mercy" (8:5). Bildad has encouraged Job that God is gracious, and that coming to him is the way to live and flourish—if only Job will confess his sin and move toward God in humility.

Job very much wants to have a talk with God, but the conversation he has in mind is different from the one Bildad is advocating. Job maintains his innocence, and instead of going to God with words of confession and repentance, he wants to *dispute* with him! He wants to establish his innocence before God. At the same time, he knows a mere mortal like himself can't just take God to court and hope to win.

Remember that in Job the speakers get many things very right about God but also say things that are *almost* right, or feel right but are wrong. Reading Job calls for entering into the perspective of each speaker while also evaluating it in light of the whole Bible. Now have someone read **Job 9:1–24** aloud, or have a few readers take turns. Then discuss the two questions below:

First evaluate Job's theology. What do you notice that he gets right about God, and what does he get wrong?

Now do an emotional evaluation. What does Job say that connects with your heart? Explain how you feel.

Finally, jump ahead to verses 32–35. Job says about God:

> "He is not a mere mortal like me that I might answer him,
> that we might confront each other in court.
> If only there were someone to mediate between us,
> someone to bring us together,
> someone to remove God's rod from me,
> so that his terror would frighten me no more.
> Then I would speak up without fear of him,
> but as it now stands with me, I cannot." (NIV)

Describe the "someone" Job longs for. What kind of person would he be, and what would he do to change the situation?

****

Now read the article, "The Impossible Conversation." Take turns by paragraph reading aloud, and then discuss the questions.

Lesson

3

ARTICLE

THE IMPOSSIBLE CONVERSATION

5 MINUTES

In his book *Just Mercy*, Bryan Stevenson tells the story of Walter McMillian, who was wrongly convicted of murder. Under public pressure to make an arrest, law enforcement officers coerced false testimony from four men who testified against McMillian. There was no evidence to corroborate their testimony, but McMillian spent six years in prison.

Imagine what that would be like. It would be terrible to be in jail. But it might be even worse to be a convicted felon, for it to be widely reported and believed by the public that you'd committed murder. You'd desperately want everyone to know it wasn't true.

Job too wants to have his day in court and set things straight. In the words of Job 13:3, "I would speak to the Almighty, and I desire to argue my case with God." Job feels condemned by God, found guilty without the benefit of so much as a conversation. So even more than relief from his suffering, Job wants vindication. He wants it to be established that he hasn't done anything wrong.

Perhaps you can relate to the experience of being judged unfairly, of people believing things about you without getting to know you or listening to you. Maybe people have prejudged you because of your ethnicity or where you're from. More generally, maybe we all can relate to some life experience of thinking, *I want things to be right between us, but I know they're not, and I don't know how to fix it.* That could apply to human relationships, and it can also apply to our relationship with God. *How can I repair things, so that there is no cloud hanging over my head? How do I get a reset?*

Job's solution is to think that if only he got a chance to talk it through with God, that would do the trick: "I have prepared my case; I know that I shall be in the right" (13:18). *Just give me a chance!* But Job's monologue here in chapter 9 also gives us two reasons why, in Job's estimation, that kind of a conversation is impossible.

The first obstacle is summarized in verse 32: "For he is not a man, as I am, that I might answer him, that we should come to trial together." It's the bottom-line takeaway from Job's reflections in the first half of the chapter. Those are lovely verses about the wisdom and power of God in creation, but the conclusion of those reflections is that God and Job are not on an equal footing. Job longs for the kind of dialogue you can have with someone you can look in the eye. And with God—well, you can't.

Verse 14 presses the point: "How then can I answer him, choosing my words with him?" And the answer is, again, that you can't. You don't. God is not like us; we are not like him. So much for that idea.

There's a second reason dialogue is impossible. Job says the reason dialogue with God won't work is because even if he could talk to God, he doesn't trust God. "If I summoned him and he answered me" [which is a big *if*], "I would not believe that he was listening to my voice. For he crushes me with a tempest and multiplies my wounds without cause" (vv. 16–17). Job says he has no reason to be sure God would play fair. Maybe this is understandable given what Job has been through. To him, God is looking capricious and temperamental. Job imagines God as chronically angry (vv. 5, 13) and even spiteful. The worst is verse 23: "When disaster brings sudden death, he mocks at the calamity of the innocent."

It's a terrible quandary. Job longs for his day in court. He wants the opportunity to converse with God. But it seems impossible. And then we come to verse 33: "If only there were someone to mediate between us, someone to bring us together" (NIV). After coming to a dead end, it's as if Job has one last what-if. *What I really need is a mediator. What if someone could speak to God on my behalf, and speak to me for him? What if this go-between could remove the terror from the relationship, so that we could just talk?*

It's a bare pencil sketch of an idea. What would that even look like? Maybe you'd doodle that sketch and then you'd look at it and say, "Oh, that's probably stupid. I'm embarrassed to show it to anyone." So you'd shove it in a drawer.

But the pencil sketch is true. In all his ranting, Job has stumbled on the key. *I need someone who is for me, who can put his hand on me. He would need to be a person like me. And what if that someone could also speak for God, could represent him somehow, could lay his hand on the divine? But who could do that but God himself?*

It all depends on this: What if God is good and kind, after all? What if *he* could provide a mediator? What if the solution to the impasse could come from him? That is exactly what has happened. That is exactly who God is—rich in mercy! He is more eager than we are to put things right between us. In the end, the initiative comes from him. And in the man he provides, we see (in flesh and blood!) the kind of God he really is.

First Timothy 2:5–6 tells us, "There is one God, and there is one mediator between God and men, the man Christ Jesus, who gave himself as a ransom for all." In the end, justification does not come about because I plead my own case so effectively. Justification comes about because a righteous Mediator sent from God pleads for me, and gives himself up to rescue me.

DISCUSSION *10 MINUTES*

What obstacles tend to keep you from having more or better conversations with God? Explain.

What kinds of experiences make you realize you need a mediator, and what kinds of experiences make you think you can do without one?

Lesson 3

EXERCISE

YOUR VIEW OF GOD

20 MINUTES

Like Job, you probably are quick to embrace some aspects of God's character and slow to believe other aspects. For this exercise, you'll consider what you believe easily and what's hard for you. For each truth about God explained below, give yourself a 5 if you are very quick to agree God is like that and to esteem him for it. Give yourself a 1 if you seldom think of God that way or tend not to value that part of who he is. You can also give a rating in between. Read and respond on your own. At the end of the exercise, you'll have a chance to share some of your findings with the group.

God is majestically ABOVE you. He is highly exalted over all things and is holy, never mixing with anything sinful or beneath him. He rules everyone with fearsome power. He "shakes the earth out of its place, and its pillars tremble" (v. 6).

O 5 I easily see and appreciate God's high-above-me distance.
O 4
O 3
O 2
O 1 I treat God as if he is hardly different from me.

God is lovingly NEAR you. In Christ, you are remade to be like God and to be with God. He delights to be at your side always, listening to you and helping you. His eternal plan is to live amid his people: "Behold, the dwelling place of God is with man" (Revelation 21:3).

O 5 I am quick to see and appreciate how God is at my side.
O 4
O 3
O 2
O 1 I suspect God is uninterested or is checking up on me from afar.

God is fiercely JUST. He will not let evil go unpunished. "In righteousness he judges and makes war" (Revelation 19:11), and you deserve to fall under his sword as he purges the world of corruption. "Can a man be pure before his Maker?" (Job 4:17).

O 5 I am highly aware of God's righteous judgment.
O 4
O 3
O 2
O 1 I act as if God easily dismisses sin.

God overflows with MERCY. He *is* love. His heart is gentle and full of compassion. Forgiveness is at the core of who he is: "a God merciful and gracious, slow to anger, and abounding in steadfast love and faithfulness" (Exodus 34:6).

O 5 I quickly believe God loves and forgives me in Christ.
O 4
O 3
O 2
O 1 I seldom really believe God could love someone like me.

God's holy grandeur shows you your NEED. There is an overwhelming gap between God and humanity, and between his purity and your pollution. You have a tremendous need for the rescue and ongoing care only God provides—and you turn in faith to Jesus.

- O 5 I strongly sense my daily need for God.
- O 4
- O 3
- O 2
- O 1 I rarely sense my neediness before God.

God's fatherly love gives you SECURITY. In Christ, God is your Father, personally. He provides for you perfectly, works all things for your good, hears all your prayers, and is giving you a heavenly home with him. You are eternally safe in his hands.

- O 5 It's easy for me to be confident of my Father's care.
- O 4
- O 3
- O 2
- O 1 It's hard for me to feel safe when I think about God.

The MEDIATOR. Now consider this: it's common to think you must find the right balance between these truths about God.

- A balance between how God is above you and how he is near you
- A balance between God's justice and his mercy
- A balance between sensing your need and feeling secure

But the gospel says God is fully all of these through Jesus the Mediator. Jesus is the glory of God who also became flesh and dwelt among us. He is how God punishes and defeats your sin, and also how he gives you mercy. You will never lose your need for him, but you are safe in him. So finish by considering how readily you appreciate Jesus.

- O 5 I often appreciate how Jesus is the Mediator Job desired.
- O 4
- O 3
- O 2
- O 1 I usually can't get very excited about Jesus.

When the group is ready, share some of your responses. How do you most easily think about God? What patterns do you see?

In what area would you most like to grow in your appreciation of God, and why?

Think about feeling needy and feeling safe. New believers often are struck by the gap between God's holiness and their sin, so that the good news of a Mediator comes as a great relief. Then as they grow in Christ, they gain an affection for God their Father. How can you preserve a deep sense that you still need Jesus even while you grow more confident that your Father loves you?

WRAP-UP AND PRAYER *10 MINUTES*

It is God who reveals himself and lets you understand him better. So as part of your prayer time, ask him to grow your appreciation for him in the areas you noted in the exercise.

Lesson

4

THE PROBLEM OF MORTALITY

BIG IDEA

In Jesus we have the hope of a resolved, uncomplicated, delightful relationship with God, unimpeded at last by sin, weakness, or death.

BIBLE CONVERSATION *20 MINUTES*

> There's an old joke. Two elderly women are at a Catskill Mountain resort, and one of 'em says, "Boy, the food at this place is really terrible." The other one says, "Yeah, I know. And such small portions." Well, that's essentially how I feel about life—full of loneliness and misery and suffering and unhappiness, and it's all over much too quickly.
>
> —Woody Allen, *Annie Hall*[1]

Much has been going on in Job's churning mind, and now his thoughts are coming out in rivers of language and imagery, chapters at a time. As we get to chapter 14, Job expresses much the same idea as Woody Allen in the quote above. Humanity is both "few of days and full of trouble." Despite the trouble of life, there's still a sharp poignancy in seeing it slip away.

Although Job is in dialogue with his friends, responding to Zophar's words in chapter 11, sometimes he seems to forget his human companions. As he expresses his wish to be able to speak to God himself, face to face, sometimes he begins to act out that longed-for conversation, looking past the friends and addressing himself to God. Have someone read **Job 14:1–17**, or have a few readers take turns. Then discuss the two questions below:

In verse 6 Job asks God to look away from people and leave them alone. What reasons might someone have for finding God's gaze unpleasant?

What do you think of Job's views about death and about life after death? (Read closely and consider both what Job expects and what he hopes might be true.)

Now read how Job's understanding about death evolves later, in **Job 19:25–27**.

> I know that my redeemer lives,
> and that in the end he will stand on the earth.
> And after my skin has been destroyed,
> yet in my flesh I will see God;
> I myself will see him
> with my own eyes—I, and not another.
> How my heart yearns within me! (NIV)

Which changes in Job's thinking most encourage you, and why?

****

Now take turns reading this lesson's article aloud, switching readers at the paragraph breaks. Then discuss the questions at the end of the article.

Lesson 4

ARTICLE

HE WILL CALL AND I WILL ANSWER

5 MINUTES

In Job 14 we get to listen in as Job stares down the specter of human mortality. He has concluded that people are like flowers that wither or shadows that flee. Verse 6 adds the image of a hired hand, a day laborer. *I'm on the clock. At the end of the day, I punch out.*

Alongside these sober reflections, Job is also trying to work out what he can discern about God's attitude toward us in our frailty. What is God's posture toward weak people who are going to die? It seems Job has begun to believe something about God that needs examination. In verse 3, Job says to God, "And do you open your eyes on such a one and bring me into judgment with you?" *God, do you scrutinize me with a critical eye? Are you a fault-finder? And are you ready to send extra trouble on anyone who seems to have it coming?*

The next thought follows naturally then: "Look away from him and leave him alone" (v. 6). *Lord, would you stop staring at me?* The life application becomes that it's best to keep your head down. Enjoy your short life in a quiet way the best you can before you die. That's what Job has begun to believe about God and about life.

But then he begins to express a hope for something better, on the other side of death. Job tries to understand his experience through the lens of what he can observe. And in nature he sees a pattern that stirs up a little hope: "For there is hope for a tree, if it be cut down, that it will sprout again" (v. 7).

Job is observant. He's seen that often new shoots grow from old tree stumps. Could there be any analogy to human experience? Job wants to hope so, but as he considers it honestly, his conclusion is no, probably not. "But a man dies and is laid low; man breathes his last, and where is he?" (v. 10). Is there any evidence in Job's world that the person who has died lives on? Not really. That person "rises not again" (v. 12). Dead is dead.

Still, listen to this language as verse 12 continues: "Till the heavens are no more he will not awake or be roused out of his sleep." Is that a way of saying there might be a time, someday, when the rules change and something new and different might be possible after all? Does it leave the door open a crack?

From there Job finds himself in the realm of *if onlys*. "If only you would hide me in the grave and conceal me till your anger has passed! If only you would set me a time and then remember me!" (v. 13 NIV). Job is imagining what it could be like in that if-only, alternative world.

Job has no reason to think that this if-only hope has any basis in reality. And yet, the way the Holy Spirit works in these speeches of Job is extraordinary. Job expresses all kinds of half-baked ideas. Not every word he says is reliable. And yet Job also expresses, out of a Holy Spirit–led imagination, authentic insights into the deepest needs of humanity. The Spirit gives him glimpses of understanding far beyond anything he could have figured out for himself.

His first idea, in verse 13, is that death could turn out to be a temporary safe place to wait out a storm. Eventually it would be safe to come out, and things would be different. God was angry then, but he's not angry now. He used to remember my sin, but now, "my transgression would be sealed up in a bag, and you would cover over my iniquity" (v. 17). The emergence on the other side of death would be a "renewal" (v. 14), something to anticipate with hope.

That's marvelous, but there's more. Remember that earlier Job wanted God to stop looking at him. Now the vision is different: "Then you will count my steps but not keep track of my sin" (v. 16 NIV). "Count my steps" means God is watching everything I do. It's personal and intimate. *God knows me!* But it's not a knowledge I shrink from; it's a knowledge I welcome.

If that is God's attitude toward me—a tender, intimate love and knowledge—then it opens up new vistas for what our relationship can be. "You would call, and I would answer you; you would long for the work of your hands" (v. 15). God who lovingly created me longs for me, and I long for my Creator. It's reciprocal! Then in chapter 19 it gets even better. What was a tentative idea is now a settled conviction:

> "I know that my redeemer lives,
> and that in the end he will stand on the earth.
> And after my skin has been destroyed,
> yet in my flesh I will see God;
> I myself will see him
> with my own eyes—I, and not another.
> How my heart yearns within me!" (vv. 25–27 NIV)

Do you dare to believe that God's posture toward you is that tender—that he would long for you? And do you dare to have stirred up in your own heart a reciprocal longing for him? Up to this point I haven't mentioned Jesus in this article, but we've been talking about Jesus all along. Jesus is the Living Redeemer, the one who by his death and resurrection makes it possible for us to stand before God after we die. Jesus embodies the attitude of God the Father toward you. He comes to earth as the overflowing abundance of the heart of God longing for you, coming not to scrutinize or accuse, but coming to save. The Redeemer stood on the earth and he will stand on it again.

In Job's imagination the hope is a future hope. God will call and you will answer. That hope can settle in your heart as a confident anticipation of what waits for you after you die. But it's not only a future hope. By God's grace it can also grow to become more of a present, lived experience. The *then* can intrude into your experience of the *now*. You can know now, if you have trusted Christ, that the posture of God toward you always is delight and affection and tenderness. And you can allow yourself a growing delight and affection toward him.

DISCUSSION *10 MINUTES*

Consider the question, "What is God's posture toward weak people who are going to die?" How do you think people you know would answer that question? What answers have you believed, either formally or in your gut?

As you live in a world full of trouble, what might you do to remember that God calls to you with longing and that in your flesh you will see God?

Lesson

EXERCISE

4

THE GAZE OF GOD

20 MINUTES

How do you feel about the idea that God sees you and takes an interest? Your answer might range from disbelief or worry to delight or wonder. And like Job, you might not have a single, simple answer. Maybe you have a confusing mix of feelings, or you hop back and forth between feelings, or your feelings have evolved over time.

On your own, read the description in each of the four boxes on the next page. They are four ways you might feel about God's gaze—the fact that his eyes are always on you. Then respond to the prompts that follow. When the group is ready, you'll discuss some of your responses.

NOTE: It's common to hold good doctrine about God, which you believe in your mind, while your daily-life gut feelings about God are different. Try to be honest about how you feel about God even if you know the "right answer" about God is something different. The space between your stated beliefs and daily feelings is good to explore.

You DOUBT God's gaze	You AVOID God's gaze
"It just doesn't seem like God is here, or interested in me at all. I'm alive now, and someday I'm going to die. That's all there is. I'm nothing after that."	"I keep my head down. I try not to do anything too bad that would make God notice me and give me trouble. Maybe after I die, he'll turn out to be lenient. But honestly, I'm nervous about him.

You WELCOME God's gaze	You RETURN God's gaze
"My only hope is for God to take notice of me. So much is wrong in the world and in me, but Jesus has amazing kindness. If his tender eyes fall on me—even *me*—I am blessed beyond all expectations."	"Jesus's love for me gives me genuine love for him. He must be so delightful to live with—far sweeter than I know now! I'm eager to know him better . . . and then better . . . and then better."

Which boxes best fit how you tend to feel about God's gaze? You might put a check mark in all the boxes that best apply.

How has your approach to God's gaze evolved over the course of your life? You might draw arrows from some boxes to others, or add other symbols to explain your movements.

What box do you desire to live in more of the time? Pick one that feels like reachable growth you can sense God might be working in you. You might draw a heart there.

When the group is ready, share and explain some of your responses.

WRAP-UP AND PRAYER *10 MINUTES*

Pray together with the knowledge that God does indeed see you and is eager to answer your prayers in ways that are immeasurably kind and good for you.

Lesson

5

THE SEARCH FOR WISDOM

BIG IDEA

Wisdom is difficult to acquire, but it can be gained through a relationship with God in Jesus.

BIBLE CONVERSATION *20 MINUTES*

After several chapters of further dispute over good behavior's connection to God's blessings, Job 28 is a change in direction. Although it's not marked off in the text with an introductory heading, its tone is a clear shift away from Job's discourse in chapters 26 and 27, which has been emotional and passionate. In general, Job's discourses are intensely personal, full of *I* and *me*. In contrast, chapter 28 seems to be above the fray, miles away from the ash heap where Job and his friends argue. There are no personal pronouns in the chapter. It's just a beautiful poem about wisdom and where to find it.

The book of Job is a clear example of wisdom literature, that ancient genre that self-consciously seeks to understand what life is about and the principles that guide it. This chapter serves as a sort of meta-intermission, self-reflective about that higher endeavor of the book. It's a step onto the patio for a breath of air before the climax of Job's story.

David Atkinson writes about this chapter, "Perhaps the time has come for some objective reflection. Perhaps we now need to stand back from this unseemly debate and think clearly. Perhaps we need a critique of both Job and his friends from the perspective of a dispassionate observer, to pause and reflect on what has been happening."[2]

As you read **chapter 28** now, be self-conscious about taking that sort of pause to reflect on the quest for wisdom, which is bigger than the book of Job. Have someone read the chapter aloud, or have several readers take turns. Then discuss the questions below:

What images in this chapter engage your imagination? Explain how they affect you.

Verse 13 says, "Man does not know [wisdom's] worth." How does the poem illustrate this in ways you've seen are true?

What stands out to you about the relationship between God and wisdom in this chapter?

****

Now take turns reading the article aloud, switching readers by paragraph. When you finish, discuss the questions that follow.

Lesson 5

ARTICLE

ASKING A BIGGER QUESTION

5 MINUTES

I like to read newspaper advice columns. People write in to ask, "Here's what's happening, I don't know what to do. Can you help me?" And the columnist offers the best advice he or she can. That's a small beginning to thinking about this passage. Now take that small beginning and expand it. Make the questions into bigger questions like: How does the world work? How do I live within it? Those questions approach the idea of *wisdom and understanding.*

Job and his friends have been arguing in circles about how best to interpret Job's suffering in light of big questions about how the world works. The tension is rising. One of the men speaks, and then another responds. *You don't know what you're talking about! Listen to me, I'll tell you, if you'll just shut your mouth.* It's unproductive.

In chapter 28 we hear another voice. Call it a Spirit-filled narrator, a voice from above the fray. This voice, rather than joining the argument, speaks to a bigger question. Where do you get wisdom? What do you have to do to obtain it? To approach an answer, he invites us first into an extended analogy.

It begins, "Surely there is a mine for silver, and a place for gold that they refine." The passage engages our imaginations, not first about wisdom, but about precious stones and metals—exquisite, hard-to-get treasures. Where do they come from? You may have never been there, but there *is* a place.

Then we're carried off into the realm of mining in the ancient world. Imagine a forgotten valley, with passageways that take you deep underground. Imagine yourself, by the light of a flickering torch, hanging from some kind of scaffold, searching out hidden veins, swinging a hammer to break precious stones out of the cave wall.

Do you want to know where gold and silver come from? *That's* where. There is such a place, for real. It's arduous, but it exists and it is possible—if you know where to look and if you have what it takes. Do you see how the writer is stirring the pot, making you want it? Can you imagine yourself on a quest to find something rare and remote and almost inaccessible? What risks would you be willing to take?

Then we read verse 12: "But where shall wisdom be found? And where is the place of understanding?" That is the real question. A place for wisdom must exist too, right? By now your heart thrills with the idea. But the sobering answer is that it's not that easy. Wisdom is even rarer than precious stones. Even if you go to remote places, "The deep says, 'It is not in me,' and the sea says, 'It is not with me.'" The sad conclusion in verse 13 is, "It is not found in the land of the living." And in case you were wondering, verse 22 says it's not in the land of the dead either.

So the tension rises. This uncommon but essential thing—this thing we must have in order to function—is not available to us. Do you feel a little anxious? A little desperate? If so, good. That's how you're supposed to feel. Life is hard, you need some handholds to navigate it—but those handholds are nowhere to be found.

So then what? "God understands the way to it, and he knows its place" (v. 23). God was there when the world came to be. He knows how it works, and he's the one you need to talk to. As we seek out a path to follow in a confusing world, Job tells us we're going to need to go through God. The closing summary of this poem's counsel is, "Behold, the fear of the Lord, that is wisdom, and to turn away from evil is understanding."

The fear of the Lord is a hard thing to explain. It refers not to a one-off encounter (give God his due and be on your way), but a settled relational posture. It's a *from here on out* way of life, the entranceway into a long and all-encompassing relationship. How do you live a life of wisdom? Let it be a life of reverent relationship with the God who knows all things. Let it be, not glib or excessively casual, but appropriately serious. Let it reflect a sense of his enormity and your smallness, his holiness and your corruption. Let his grand goodness attract your heart, as something not to shrink from, but to draw near to, like a bonfire on a cold night. Let your whole, trembling self be captured by the God who welcomes you into a lifetime of relationship with him.

We also need a wider-angle, whole-Bible perspective on all of this. Because the testimony of the whole Bible is not just that wisdom is found generally in relationship with God. The more specific message is that the wisdom of God is particularly discovered in relationship with God the Son, Jesus Christ.

The New Testament says some extraordinary things about Jesus, including John 1:3. "All things were made through him, and without him was not any thing made that was made." With that ringing in your ears, read Job 28:25–27 again.

> "When he gave to the wind its weight
> and apportioned the waters by measure,
> when he made a decree for the rain
> and a way for the lightning of the thunder,

> then he saw it and declared it;
>
> he established it, and searched it out."

Where Job describes God weighing out the wind, making a decree for the rain, it is speaking about Jesus! In 1 Corinthians 1:24, the apostle Paul calls Christ "the wisdom of God." The Son, uniquely in the Trinity, is the expression of wisdom. He is the one in whom all things come together and make sense. Jesus is quantum-mechanics wisdom: the person of Jesus, both God and man, is what makes impossible-to-reconcile things reconcilable. When you throw up your hands at the difficulty of the problem, Jesus is the answer at the back of the book.

You can travel the world and get a raft of credentials. But to find wisdom, the only way is in a relationship with God through Jesus Christ.

DISCUSSION *10 MINUTES*

How have you felt desperate to find wisdom and understanding, like Job 28 describes? Or when have you seen it in others?

How do you keep a long-term fear of the Lord (a reverent relationship with Jesus) even when you don't feel like engaging with him at times?

Lesson 5

EXERCISE

WISDOM TREASURE MAP

The images in Job 28 give you a way to picture your lifelong search for godly wisdom. For this exercise, you will "map out" some of your desires for wisdom by writing them as treasures on a treasure map. On your own, read through all the treasure-map instructions below, and then sketch your map. You'll tell the group about your map when you're finished.

WISDOM TREASURE MAP INSTRUCTIONS

Put some ENGAGE-WITH-JESUS treasures on your map. What times and activities are the gems in your relationship with Christ? How do you hear his word? When do you speak to him? How do you discover and enjoy all his beauty—from his majesty as Creator to his tenderness as your Savior? Think of ways you already have these times of renewal with Jesus, and of new precious times you would like to add. Be specific, and write a few ways to engage with Jesus on your map, as if they were hidden veins of gold. To get into the treasure-map spirit, you might mark each of them with a scrawled X.

Also include some LOVE-OTHER-PEOPLE treasures. Job 28 ends by saying wisdom is found by turning from evil. You turn from evil by *loving other people*: "The wisdom from above . . . is full of mercy and good fruits" (James 3:17). So how might you set aside selfishness and take on a quest to care for others? Where do you see jewels of loving service in your life—now or in the future? They may be as near as the people you live with or as distant as world missions. Include a few specific ways to love others on your treasure map.

Include the terrain. Both kinds of treasure (engaging with Jesus and loving others) can be hard to get. So sketch out your map in a way that illustrates the difficulties you expect as you pursue your treasures. Include mountains, canyons, caves, or even dragons. Which treasures feel tough for you to reach, like they are hidden amid these obstacles? Draw your map, and arrange your treasures in it, to depict this.

Consider your route. A wisdom-hunting life requires both kinds of treasure, because engaging with Jesus and loving others build on each other. As you get to know Jesus's love for you, you will grow a passion to go out and love others. And the challenge of loving others will in turn keep driving you back to Jesus for his comfort and encouragement. So construct your map in a way that lets you mine for both kinds of treasure, never straying far from either.

Now sketch out your wisdom treasure map.

When the group is ready, explain your wisdom treasure map. What gems are you eager to add to your life? How will you search them out, and what obstacles feel in your way?

WRAP-UP AND PRAYER *10 MINUTES*

Pray for each other and your desires to seek out wisdom.

Lesson

6

LOSING EVERYTHING

BIG IDEA

Our personal stories of loss and sorrow find meaning and hope in Jesus's bigger story of loss and sorrow.

BIBLE CONVERSATION *20 MINUTES*

We are approaching the end of the book of Job, and Job the innocent sufferer is running out of things to say. There will come a point, soon now, after many chapters of emotion and argument, when the defense will finally rest and Job will close his mouth. His friends, too, will have said all they know to say. But before Job concludes, he makes one last speech. The tone of chapters 29 and 30 is less defiant and more sorrowful. Job sadly remembers the life he once enjoyed and contrasts it with his present experience. He numbers his losses, lingers over his memories, and grieves deeply.

Have someone read **Job 29:1–12 and 30:1–10**, or have a few readers take turns. As you read or listen, allow yourself space to remember losses in your own life—things you enjoyed in the past that are no longer part of your experience. Then discuss the questions below:

Look again at chapter 29, and imagine yourself living Job's former life before his sufferings. What about that life stands out to you, and why?

Now imagine yourself living Job's later life in chapter 30. Who are your new neighbors, and how do you feel about your life with them?

Tell about a time in your life that you enjoyed "the friendship of God" (29:4) in an especially sweet way, or about a time it felt absent. What was that like?

****

Now read the article aloud, taking turns by paragraph, and discuss the questions that follow.

Lesson

6

ARTICLE

THAT WAS THEN, THIS IS NOW

5 MINUTES

Every one of us has suffered loss of one kind or another. At one time you enjoyed something that was, for a while, part of the package of your daily life. It may have been a home or a job, a relationship or a community. Perhaps there was a time of life that was especially sweet. Maybe you loved your college days, or you loved being the parent of young children. Perhaps you feel a wistful nostalgia as you look back on that time. Those things were good and pleasant. They made you happy. But now that time is gone.

There's a wide range of experiences that fall into the category of loss. Some of them are sudden or truly tragic—the saddest stories you've ever heard. Many of them are much more ordinary or gradual. But every story of loss is a sad story. This passage in Job is that kind of story. Job has suffered tremendous loss, and here he takes time to remember.

In chapter 29, Job remembers that for a long time his life went really well. He was a golden child, and everything he touched seemed to flourish. Verse 6 gives us the perfect metaphor: "My steps were washed with butter." And with these good circumstances came the sense that God was near: "The friendship of God was upon my tent" (v. 4).

It's a simple theology—understanding blessing on your life as evidence that God is with you and is watching over you. It's the same simple theology that is assumed by everybody throughout the book of Job. It can be problematic, for sure, but it communicates our common lived experience. Maybe you've said something similar yourself when things were going well in your life. *God is really with me. He's blessing us!*

But it's all past tense. When Job laments about how the Almighty was with him, the implication is that God isn't near anymore. Job's children are gone. The butter has dried up. He's over the hill. And honestly, it stinks.

The rest of the chapter is a remembrance of who Job once was in his community. He was a prominent citizen, universally respected. Everybody spoke well of him. Reading through this section, it's almost as if Job himself can scarcely believe it: *My goodness, I really was somebody!*

Have you ever been looked up to? Have you ever been a big fish, even in a small pond or for a short time? Have you received awards and gotten promotions? Job was a big fish. He's not making it up; it was all real. But it's over. That was then, and this is now.

Chapter 30 unpacks the *this is now*: "But now they laugh at me" (v. 1). Job has come down in life. This wise and good man, who was once so loved by his community, is now literally on the ash heap outside the city wall. Not only is he not a prominent citizen, he has no place in the community at all.

In this ancient town was a class of people who lived on the margin. They were ignorant and vulgar, "driven out from human company" (v. 5) because of their behavior and way of life. In the world Job now inhabits, he has become less than them. The kids on the edge of town make up dirty jokes and songs, and Job is the punchline. "They abhor me; they keep aloof from me; they do not hesitate to spit at the sight of me" (v. 10). That tells you all you need to know. There's the *that was then*, and there's the *this is now*.

Engaging this passage requires us to stop and look and listen to the one who has come down in life. That's uncomfortable! Our instinct is to avert our eyes, because it's frightening to think that what you have might not be yours to keep. It's frightening that someone who was doing so well could come down with such a bump. What awful story have we wandered into? And how do we get out?

Have you ever thought of Jesus as one who experienced loss? Second Corinthians 8:9 says, "Though he was rich, yet for your sake he became poor, so that you by his poverty might become rich." Jesus existed together with the Father in light and bliss and glory—until he suffered an astounding loss. Unlike Job, his loss did not come upon him as a sudden blow of misfortune. He chose it, with his eyes open, willingly. He was "in the form of God," but "made himself nothing" (Philippians 2:6 ESV, 7 NIV). In the end the vulgar, violent men of his day not only laughed at him and spat on him, they brutalized him. They hung him on a cross to die.

Every story of loss—Job's, yours, and mine—must intersect with that story of loss. When you're inside your own story—when *that was then, this is now* is your present lived experience—one question becomes very important: What will be? Job gives us a glimpse of the future. The book's last chapter is about restoration. It says, "The LORD blessed the latter days of Job more than his beginning" (42:12). For all the strangeness of that chapter, we need to fight to hear its good ending. A better ending. Restoration and then some.

Job's ending points to our better ending in Jesus. He who was crucified was also raised and exalted. He won a decisive victory that guarantees the full redemption of all things. It's now just a matter of time. If you have trusted in Jesus—if your story is tethered to his—then God is with you in the present and redeeming your future.

DISCUSSION *10 MINUTES*

What feelings stick with you when you stop, look, and listen to Job in his profound experience of loss?

How are the losses you have suffered in life similar to those of Job, or of Jesus?

Lesson

6

EXERCISE

LOWS AND HIGHS OF JESUS

10 MINUTES

The life story of Jesus has two main parts: (1) he stooped low and suffered, and (2) he is raised high in glory. A believer in Jesus shares this same life pattern. You pass through many losses in your current life on the way to your full glory. And during this time of loss, both parts of Jesus's life are meant to encourage you—both how he too suffered loss to be near you, and how in him you are assured of great gain.

On your own, read through the descriptions of how Jesus stooped low (marked by a down arrow), and how he is raised high and you will be too (marked by an up arrow). Then answer the questions, which ask you to pick between them by marking a down or up arrow in the box beside each question. Although you are meant to be encouraged by *both* Jesus's lows and his highs, being forced to pick between them can help you see the value of both and how they function in your life. You'll share some of your results when you finish.

How Jesus stooped low

Jesus didn't just suffer in your place all the punishment from God you deserve for your sin; he also suffered *alongside you* all the pains, indignities, sadness, and unfairness of life in this world. No one else has suffered loss to the degree he did. To be your Savior, he emptied himself of his divine glory and lived as a servant. He was abandoned by friends, betrayed, persecuted, and treated shamefully. "Surely he has borne our griefs and carried our sorrows" (Isaiah 53:4).

How Jesus is raised high (and you will be too)

Jesus is risen from the dead, ascended to heaven, seated to reign, and coming in glory. Spiritually, you are already alive too and seated with him. You are awaiting your perfect and sinless body, final vindication, and eternal happiness on the day he returns. "For the powers of the heavens will be shaken. And then they will see the Son of Man coming in a cloud with power and great glory. Now when these things begin to take place, straighten up and raise your heads, because your redemption is drawing near" (Luke 21:26–28).

Which do you find **easiest to believe is true**: how fully Jesus stooped low or how fully he (and you with him) is raised high? Put a down arrow in the box for how Jesus stooped low, or an up arrow for how he is raised high.

Which **most sounds like good news** to you when you hear it? Mark a down arrow for how Jesus stooped low, or an up arrow for how he is raised high.

Which **most makes you want to know Jesus better**, or instills in you a love for him? Mark a down arrow for how Jesus stooped low, or an up arrow for how he is raised high.

Which sounds like it can be **most encouraging or helpful** during times when you are suffering? Mark a down arrow for how Jesus stooped low, or an up arrow for how he is raised high.

Which makes you **most eager to tell someone else** about it? Mark a down arrow for how Jesus stooped low, or an up arrow for how he is raised high.

When the group is ready, share some of your responses. Tell where you marked down or up arrows, and explain why.

What patterns or tendencies do you notice? Are there ways Jesus feels especially precious to you, or ways he could start to feel more precious?

WRAP-UP AND PRAYER *10 MINUTES*

For your closing prayer time together, remember again the importance of lament. If you feel a sense of loss, tell your Father about it.

Lesson

7

THE PROBLEM OF INJUSTICE

BIG IDEA

Jesus is both the ultimate innocent man who does not get what he deserves and also the one God vindicates. Any injustice in our stories is redeemed when it's wrapped in his story.

BIBLE CONVERSATION *20 MINUTES*

Through most of the book, Job has been in dialogue with three friends. They've been going back and forth, trying to make sense together out of the extraordinary suffering that has fallen on Job. It has not been a fruitful conversation. The friends simply cannot conceive of the idea that Job's suffering has not been in some way the just payment for his sins, but Job continues to insist that he is innocent.

In chapter 32, a fourth friend speaks for the first time. He is Elihu, a younger man, who has been listening to the whole conversation and growing increasingly angry. He's angry at Job for his stubborn self-justification, and he's angry with Eliphaz, Bildad, and Zophar for their inability to demonstrate that Job is in the wrong. Elihu is bursting to have his turn to speak, and to set all the older men straight. As it turns out, Elihu has little new to say. He essentially rehashes the other friends' arguments. But he speaks with an extra dose of self-confident self-righteousness. Elihu believes he is speaking up for God and taking a last stand for what's right.

Have someone read **Job 34:1–12** aloud. Then discuss the questions below:

What makes Elihu so angry with Job? In what ways does he understand Job accurately, and in what ways does he mischaracterize him?

What does Elihu believe about God? How is he right about God, and what does he say that's problematic?

People sometimes struggle with the idea that "God would do wrong" (v. 12 NIV). When have you doubted God's goodness, or when have you seen friends or family members struggle in this way?

****

Now read the article aloud, taking turns by paragraph, and discuss the questions that follow.

Lesson

7

ARTICLE

GETTING WHAT YOU DESERVE

5 MINUTES

One Sunday afternoon a dog got loose in our neighborhood and bit the little boy next door. The whole block was dismayed. The next day I was talking with the boy's father, who was sad and angry. He said to me, "He didn't deserve this."

He didn't deserve this. Why do we feel that needs to be said? It seems many people instinctively want to believe in a kind of pop-culture version of karma, that how you live should work itself out in what you get back. The kid was just a boy playing in the yard on a spring day. What happened to him wasn't right.

The problem with that idea is that our experience does not bear it out. Notably, bad things often seem to happen to people who don't have it coming. Nevertheless, the idea is hard to shake. Even today, there seems to be an implicit assumption that if you suffer, you've probably brought it upon yourself—so if that's not the case, we feel the need to say so.

Elihu is a confident young man. He's a black-and-white thinker with little tolerance for gray. He berates Job, imposing on Job's experience of suffering a grid of interpretation that flows from what Elihu believes about God and humanity: "For according to the work of a man [God] will repay him, and according to his ways he will make it befall him" (v. 11). Elihu believes there is a discernible, immediate, divine cause and effect connecting a person's behavior and his or her circumstances. Suffering indicates sin. If Elihu were talking to my neighbor, he'd say the kid must have had it coming. If you're poor, sick, or disabled, you'd better repent or it's only going to get worse.

And according to Elihu, if you question that simple cause-and-effect understanding of suffering, you're saying God is unjust. Against that simplistic read on life, Job speaks his experience: *Look, I've always tried to do right, but this is what happened to me.* Elihu hears Job's testimony, and it alarms him. *Are you saying that God is capricious, that God is unpredictable? That can't be!* "Far be it from God that he should do wickedness" (v. 10). *Job, you need to shut your mouth.*

It's a standoff. On the one hand we have the conviction that a good God is ruling over the details of the world with justice, and on the other we have the lived experience of a truthful man. The two should be able to exist together in tension with one another, but what we find is that the friends are very uncomfortable with Job's lived experience. They try to shut down his testimony. They effectively tell him that he has not experienced what he knows he has. It's an ancient gaslighting session—constant pressure to make Job doubt what he knows is true.

So where do we go from here? We need to take our lived experience, and Job's lived experience, and hold them together with the lived experience of Jesus.

Think again about that phrase: *He didn't deserve this.* The gospel writers each make that exact point about Jesus. For instance, in Matthew 27:23, Pilate asks, "What evil has he done?" In Luke 23:41, one of the criminals hanging next to Jesus says to the other, "We are receiving the due reward of our deeds, but this man has done nothing wrong."

It's the drumbeat of the narrative: *Jesus has done nothing wrong—but this is what he gets.* What would Elihu say to Jesus?

But there is another part to Jesus's story. On the third day he rose again from the dead. Part of what the resurrection means is the *vindication* of Jesus. In his resurrection Jesus is cleared of wrongdoing—publicly acquitted. The Father himself declares. "He didn't deserve this!" The injustice is undone and Jesus *gets what he deserves.* He ascends to glory and receives the worship of the nations.

Part of our human experience is that there are very real occasions when we do not get what we deserve. We act in good conscience and make good choices, but we receive back disrespect and abuse and unfair treatment. That happens. That's happened to you. And in the midst of that you say, "I don't deserve this." Jesus's experience can hold and validate that experience.

But overall, is that a fair summary of my life in total—that I am generally a good person but receive back worse than I deserve? I know that for myself, that's not the case. The reality is that my life has been characterized from top to bottom by unmerited blessing. I'm a sinner who's been shown much grace and much mercy, both in my ordinary circumstances and all the more in Christ.

Elihu is complicated. Some things he says are problematic, but other things are quite lovely. His assumption that Job has some serious secret sins is unwarranted. But if it had been true, the advice Elihu gives is actually good advice. In chapter 33 he tells Job not to be afraid but to confess his sins and repent, and God will respond with mercy.

Those verses are full of grace and truth. Elihu says:

> "Someone may be chastened on a bed of pain
> with constant distress in their bones....
> Yet if there is an angel at their side...
> and he is gracious to that person and says to God,

> 'Spare them from going down to the pit;
> I have found a ransom for them—
> let their flesh be renewed like a child's . . .'
> then that person can pray to God and find favor with him. . . .
> And they will go to others and say,
> 'I have sinned, I have perverted what is right,
> but I did not get what I deserved.
> God has delivered me from going down to the pit,
> and I shall live to enjoy the light of life.'" (33:19–28 NIV)

That's the life story of every Christian: I sinned and perverted what was right, but I did not get what I deserved. My story is not primarily a story of undeserved suffering; it's primarily a story of undeserved grace.

DISCUSSION *10 MINUTES*

When you encounter undeserved suffering, how do you process it? What arguments, clashing ideas, or standoffs do you find yourself dealing with?

When you look at the world, are you quicker to notice undeserved suffering or undeserved mercy? What about when you look at your own life, or the lives of people you love? Explain.

Lesson 7

EXERCISE

REASONS TO LOVE AND SERVE

20 MINUTES

The many angles the Bible gives you for looking at injustice aren't just an exercise in deep thought. They also give you multiple reasons to *do* justice. In this exercise, you will consider how the gospel of Jesus and his justice propel you out on mission, telling about him and loving others.

On your own, read through each of the truths about God's justice that are explained below along with a section of biblical poetry about each. For each truth, pick a line or two from the poetry that you find especially meaningful or encouraging. You might circle, underline, or otherwise mark that line (or lines). Make it something that helps to propel you out, giving you eagerness to do good and work for Jesus's kingdom. When you finish, you'll tell the group about the lines you selected and why you chose them.

TRUTH #1: A good life is generally good for you and others. Elihu is partly right. God has created this world according to his justice, and living by that justice tends to work out. Life as a self-serving liar and thief usually leads to trouble. But a truthful and generous life lets you thrive, generally—and it pushes back injustice in the world. Despite evil, persecution, and hardships, love for others and service to God often brings many rewards.

> What man is there who desires life
>   and loves many days, that he may see good?
> Keep your tongue from evil
>   and your lips from speaking deceit.
> Turn away from evil and do good;
>   seek peace and pursue it. (Psalm 34:12–14)

TRUTH #2: Justice wins in the end. Even if you don't see it immediately, Jesus will prevail over evil in the long run. Human history is marked by apparently senseless suffering, but the King will make it right when he returns. His resurrection is proof of this, and of your own resurrection. You can serve God "knowing that in the Lord your labor is not in vain" (1 Corinthians 15:58). It brings glory and honor that will last eternally.

> Your name, O Lord, endures forever,
>   your renown, O Lord, throughout all ages.
> For the Lord will vindicate his people
>   and have compassion on his servants. (Psalm 135:13–14)

TRUTH #3: You actually get what you *don't* deserve. It turns out your vindication will not be due at all to your own good life, and your service to God will not be enough to save you. You are treasured only because of *Jesus's* good life and his sacrifice for your sins, and your connection to him. This means the pressure is off. You can go out and love others even knowing you will often fail, and do this without fear of condemnation or loss of self-worth. And you can tell others about this freedom too.

> "To give knowledge of salvation to his people
>   in the forgiveness of their sins,

because of the tender mercy of our God,
    whereby the sunrise shall visit us from on high
to give light to those who sit in darkness and in the shadow of death,
    to guide our feet into the way of peace." (Luke 1:77–79)

TRUTH #4: By doing right, you please God. Even though your good works are in no way a counterbalance to make up for your sin, in God's economy your choices to seek what is good do matter. Though tainted by sin and weakness, your service to God is washed and made acceptable as you do it in Christ, who is making you his spotless bride. He loved you first, and now your responding acts of love for God and others delight him. He will honor them when the time is right.

"Let us rejoice and exult
    and give him the glory,
for the marriage of the Lamb has come,
    and his Bride has made herself ready;
it was granted her to clothe herself
    with fine linen, bright and pure"—
for the fine linen is the righteous deeds of the saints.
(Revelation 19:7–8)

When the group is ready, share some of what you noted. What truths about God's justice make you eager to *do* justice, love others, and tell about Jesus? Explain why. If there are specific ways you might put that eagerness to work, tell about them too.

WRAP-UP AND PRAYER *10 MINUTES*

As you close with a time of prayer, ask your Father to make you eager to do justice even amid injustice you experience.

Lesson

8

WORDS FROM THE WHIRLWIND

BIG IDEA

In a world that is often perplexing, there's much we don't know or understand. But in Christ the mystery of what God is doing turns out to be much better than we could have guessed.

BIBLE CONVERSATION *25 MINUTES*

Most of the book of Job is a series of speeches, or discourses, by Job and his four friends. But the final word is reserved for God. God does not wade into the human argument. He doesn't answer questions or speak to the issues raised by the human speakers. He leaves a lot mysterious and unclarified. Notably, he never explains why Job is suffering!

It may be difficult for us to receive God's words. In fact, some have found this last discourse deeply frustrating. As you read, be prepared for the idea that God might speak not to your intellectual questions but to your heart. There may be things more important for you to hear than explanations. In these chapters, God speaks across the gap between the human and the divine. He speaks to us in our mortality, our finitude, and our weakness.

Before you read, ask someone in your group to pray for grace for you to inhabit that space and hear what God has to say. Ideally, if you can take the time, read **chapters 38–42:6 of Job** in their entirety, allowing the words to wash over you as you listen. The rest of the lesson has been shortened to give you time for this. Or if that feels like too much, ask four readers to read these portions aloud one after the other: **Job 38:1–7; 39:5–12; 41:1–11; and 42:1–3**. Then discuss the questions below:

What might be the emotional impact of these chapters on Job, or what is it on you?

Scan the passage for questions, and see if you can classify them into types. How might it feel to be asked each type of question?

****

Now take turns reading the article aloud. Then discuss the questions at the end.

Lesson 8

ARTICLE

WHAT YOU DON'T KNOW

5 MINUTES

For thirty-seven chapters, Job has been suffering, and he has been talking. Out of his tremendous loss has flowed an abundance of words. But now the time for words is over. Now God says it's enough. Because what Job doesn't realize, despite all his words, is that he doesn't know what he's talking about!

It's actually a remarkable expression of grace: Job cries out, *and God answers him*. The God of Job is transcendent, but he is also relational. God may not answer Job's questions, but he answers *him*.

The first thing God does is to tell Job what all his talking amounts to. It's just "words without knowledge." Then, to deliver that to his heart, God proceeds to ask Job one question after another. He asks questions about the natural world—the heavens and the deep. In sum: Can you explain how the universe works? But rather than asking one or two general questions, God asks many specific ones. The questions expose Job's ignorance. They show him how much he hasn't seen and doesn't understand.

In chapter 39, the focus of the questions shifts. To enter into this portion, imagine you live in a society that does not have cars or computers, but it does have lots of goats and donkeys and camels. Your life is lived at the edge of wild places, but those wild places are largely unknown to you. Your information about the animals that live there is scanty.

Now listen as God asks Job questions about wild animals, and as he describes their behavior. The discourse highlights the difference between the domesticated animals Job knows well and these wild animals that are mysterious to him. God talks about the wild donkey and the wild ox. They are related to the donkeys and oxen Job knows, but these beasts are wild. The donkey "hears not the shouts of the driver. He ranges the mountains as his pasture" (39:7–8).

What is Job supposed to hear? I think God wants Job to ponder the idea of wildness: Job, do you know anything about the wild donkey? He lives his whole life way out in the wilderness. He does what he wants. He goes where he wants. He doesn't care what you think. And how about the wild ox? Can you domesticate him? Could you just go out and whistle, and he'll trot on over, and you can throw a rope over him and hook him up to your plow? Good luck with that! The wild ox does not answer to you.

Then the climax of the zoology lesson: God talks about Behemoth and Leviathan. Don't worry about identifying exactly what kind of animals they might be. The point is that they are big and strong and most definitely undomesticated! It's the same message, times a thousand. Behemoth wallows in the marsh, with only his nostrils showing, and he doesn't give two hoots about you. And Leviathan is terrifying! What God says is actually quite funny: "Will you play with him as with a bird, or will you put him on a leash for your girls?" (41:5).

The overall effect is: Job, it's time to know your place. This world of hailstorms and lightning, of mountain goats and monsters—this world keeps on spinning without reference to you. The world does not dance to your tune or offer you explanations for its actions. You can't make it play by your rules.

And if that is true about the creation, how much more is it true about the Creator? Where Job perceives injustice, could that be because he only sees the smallest slice of the whole? Job has underestimated God's wisdom, which comprehends a myriad of things beyond Job's imagination. God answers Job's indignation by peeling back the curtain just a bit on the breadth of the things known to him but unknown to Job.

There's wisdom to be found even in that, understanding that you're not as smart as you thought. But again, we need more. In the New Testament, as the apostles speak and write about Jesus and the events of his life, death, and resurrection, there's an element to their perspective that is different from our own. It's the element of *surprise*. As the apostles talk about Jesus, there's a sense of wonder and lingering amazement. There's the sense that nobody saw him coming. They had no idea. The best guess of the prophets was only kind of like the real, actual person. What has happened in Christ is all just miles better than anyone had dared to hope.

Paul writes from that perspective in Romans 11:33. "Oh, the depths of the riches and wisdom and knowledge of God! How unsearchable are his judgments and how inscrutable his ways!" It's precisely the lesson Job needed to learn.

But in what way are God's ways inscrutable? In this way: they are better than you think. God is wiser than you think, kinder than you think. The things you don't know are *wonderful*. When we're perplexed, angry, and baffled by our circumstances, our wild and undomesticated God is working out good purposes toward the redemption of all things. "No eye has seen, nor ear heard, nor the heart of man imagined, what God has prepared for those who love him" (1 Corinthians 2:9).

The book of Job teaches us not to be simplistic or facile in our working theology. We can't always make things make sense, and we mustn't be ham-handed in the way we answer other people's suffering with cliches. But this we know: the story of Jesus is one of suffering before it is one of glory.

In Jesus Christ we learn about the love of God and his determination to redeem his broken world. There's a lot that I don't know, but what I know about Jesus persuades me that the Father has loved me more than I ever knew. And I'm emboldened to believe that he is working good for me, even here and even now. In Christ my story is caught up in a larger story. And in that larger story, suffering is being swallowed up in redemption.

DISCUSSION *10 MINUTES*

When have you been confronted with your own lack of understanding about God? What was that like?

How can you cultivate a posture of humility about what you do not know?

Lesson 8

EXERCISE

BETTER THAN YOU THINK

15 MINUTES

For all their wisdom and knowledge about God, Job and his friends still could not fathom God's greatness. The same is true of us. Our minds can't grasp the vastness of God's full beauty, and our hearts may remain skeptical even of truths we do understand about God. Whatever excellent theological learning you might have, or whatever nearness to God you might enjoy, he's even better than you think.

On your own, read through the list of better-than-you-think statements about God. They are drawn from this lesson and previous lessons in this study. Pick one statement (or create your own) that encourages you, or one you want to remember more often. Use that statement as you fill in the blanks in the rest of the exercise. When you finish, you'll be able to share your responses with the group.

HOW GOD IS BETTER THAN YOU THINK (pick one to consider)

- ☐ God is **kinder** than I think.
- ☐ God is **wiser** than I think.

- ☐ God is **stronger** than I think.
- ☐ God is **more generous** than I think.
- ☐ God is **more invested in me** than I think.
- ☐ God is **more forgiving** than I think.
- ☐ God is **a closer companion** than I think.
- ☐ God is ______________________________ than I think.

Now that you have picked one way God is better than you think, ponder it by filling in the blanks below. Put the quality of God you picked in the first blank. In the second blank, write a creative image from nature that shows how it is beyond your understanding. For example, Job might write: "God is wiser than I think. He is beyond what I know, like all the boundaries of the oceans."

God is ____________________ than I think. He is beyond what I know, like ____.

Although God's glory is beyond you, you have a way to see it that Job did not have as he pondered God's word: "The Word became flesh and dwelt among us, and we have seen his glory, glory as of the only Son from the Father, full of grace and truth" (John 1:14). When you read and hear about the life of Jesus, you start to see what is beyond seeing. So in the first blank below, again write the quality of God you picked. In the second blank, write something amazing about how Jesus lived that lets you start to see God's vast beauty.

God is ____________________ than I think. I start to see this when I look at how Jesus ____.

When the group is ready, share some of your responses. What did you select, and why?

How might you live differently if you became more certain that God really is good in that way, and is working in ways you cannot see?

WRAP-UP AND PRAYER *10 MINUTES*

As you pray together, include praise and thanks to God for his goodness beyond understanding. You might also discuss what your group will do now that this study is over.

LEADER'S NOTES

These notes give thoughts and background information that connect to each lesson and its discussion questions. The discussion leader should read these notes before the study begins. Sometimes, after the group has first searched out the passage for itself, the leader may want to refer participants to a point found here.

LESSON 1: MEET THE INNOCENT SUFFERER

It's common for modern Western people to have a negative gut-level reaction to the narrative bookends of Job. Why would God apparently so lightly pull the rug out from under a good man who worshiped and feared him? The dialogue between God and Satan might read as a bizarre bet at the expense of real people. And the "all better now" of chapter 42's conclusion often rings hollow too.

These are dilemmas the people in your group need to be able to discuss and wrestle with, but ones the book itself does not really address. In fact, it's fair to ask whether the details of the poetic dialogue in Job, and even the details in the narrative frame, are meant to be taken as historical record. We can ask this even though we are committed to the Bible's authority. The Scriptures do seem to tell us Job was a real, historical figure who lived righteously, suffered much, and remained steadfast (see Ezekiel 14:14; James 5:11). But he is a figure of antiquity (Job 42:16 places him in the Genesis era of long lifespans), and the book's genre is wisdom literature, not historical narrative. The author of Job, inspired by the Spirit, apparently makes use of an old story as a context for exploring issues of suffering, godliness, and reward.

For readers of every time and place, the narrative forces us to enter into a disturbing disconnect between the kind of man Job is and the suffering he experiences. The story is *meant* to be appalling. It's meant to raise questions of fairness and whether there can be, in Job's universe, any kind of cause-and-effect relationship between how one lives and the blessings or curses that follow. Chapters 1 and 2 stir up those questions but do not answer them. Instead, they give us a story to hold in our hearts and ponder.

LESSON 2: LAMENT FROM THE ASH HEAP

The first ten verses of chapter 3 are about Job in anguish over the things that have happened to him. He "opened his mouth" (v. 1) in the hearing of his friends, and he curses the day of his birth. Job goes on a rant. He goes round and round on this theme. It would have been hard to listen to. But it all boils down to, *It would have been better if I had never been born.* Job's birth ushered him into a life that would be characterized by a deeper trouble than anyone had seen before. The language of verse 10 is important. Job says the day of his birth "did not shut the doors of my mother's womb, nor hide trouble from my eyes." He means he was not sheltered from trouble. For him, suffering is not an academic concept. He's seen it with his own eyes.

And in that mental space, Job begins to entertain a romanticized idea of what it would be like to be dead. He latches onto the scenario that he might have been stillborn. Tragically, that strikes him as the best-case scenario for his life. What's the appeal? When you're dead you can rest. When you're dead your problems resolve themselves. "Then I would have lain down and been quiet; I would have slept; then I would have been at rest" (v. 13). To Job it sounds lovely. At this moment, that's what he believes. (Not everything Job says in this book is reliable or wise.)

Bear in mind that some in your group may have had a season of life in which they, too, fantasized about death or even considered suicide (which Job never seems to do). Others may have experienced the loss of a child who died in the womb or shortly after birth. This is a "handle with care" passage. Enter it prayerfully, and be attentive to the Holy Spirit as you listen to people discuss what they read. But know too that the Spirit may use passages like these to do a surprisingly helpful work in the hearts of his people.

If people in your group share things that are raw and personal, don't feel the need to correct them or sanitize what they share. Don't try to fix a complex and painful life experience; it's okay to leave things a little messy and unresolved. If someone expresses a present desire for self-harm, do take that seriously and follow up after the meeting to ensure they have the needed mental health support.

LESSON 3: A DAY IN COURT

Implicit in our discussion of Job 9 is the tension between the truth that God is immanent (near to us) and the truth that he is transcendent (exalted and holy). Job has very little understanding of God as immanent, but he is articulate about his transcendence: "His wisdom is profound, his power is vast" (9:4 NIV). But in his transcendence, God to Job is also unapproachable. Relationship with him seems impossible. God inspires awe, but really not love. In Job's mind God becomes capricious, unkind, and volatile—which he is not. But what Job gets profoundly right is the *differentness* of God: "He is not a mere mortal like me" (9:32 NIV). As God says in Isaiah 55:9, "As the heavens are higher than the earth, so are my ways higher than your ways and my thoughts than your thoughts."

Job is right that God is not like us. He is right that human beings cannot approach him as equals. Job rightly perceives the need for a Mediator, and in his way actually models a kind of almost-faith that God might provide that Mediator. And yet there is a huge gap between Job's vague idea and the reality of Christ. Reading this text gives us a fresh knowledge of how shocking the incarnation is, how marvelously God has "colored in" the bare outline that Job saw dimly.

But what do we do with verses like 9:16–18 or 23, in which Job says things about God that are contrary to his character? This is one of the challenges of the book—not everything Job says, or that his friends say, is reliable. But it's not always unreliable, either! How do we know if Job, or his friends, are understanding God and his purposes correctly, or if they are misrepresenting him? It will help to place their words into a larger biblical perspective. Remember that we as readers have much more information about what was happening to Job than he himself does in the midst of it. We know about the spiritual warfare that has happened in chapter 1, and we know what God will do and say at the end of the book. Job, compared to us as readers, is speaking in the dark. It's important, too, to keep in mind that although Scripture tells one unified story, that story comes to us in sixty-six separate books, each with unique authors, settings, and literary styles. We've noted that the story of Job happens early in the chronology of the Bible's overall story; Job himself has no Bible at all! God's revelation of himself is *progressive*: over time, much more about God's character, love, steadfastness, and power will be revealed—along with the ultimate redemption and restoration of his fallen world through the coming of Christ. But Job knows very little of all this. We read his story in light of things revealed to us but not to him. Job will get more light at the end of the book than he has before that point in the narrative, and that "more light" in chapters 38–42 is crucial to the proper interpretation of the book as a whole. As God ultimately reveals himself directly to Job, and as he reveals himself in the rest of Scripture, we are assured that what we know about God is accurate—because it comes directly from God himself.

LESSON 4: THE PROBLEM OF MORTALITY

The themes of this lesson lead to a question you might listen for between the lines as participants discuss Job 14. If you are a believer in Jesus, what is God's attitude toward you? Most people's answers fall into one of two columns. Column A: God is disappointed in me, critical, and disapproving. Column B: God is delighted with me, warm, and full of compassion.

Even if we know that the answers in column B are true, for many of us it's hard to settle there long-term. We keep defaulting back to a nagging feeling that column A is still *more* true. Job 14 includes both the idea of a critical, scrutinizing God, and a God who longs for the ones he has created. For those who are in Christ, the delighted-with-me God is the right answer. But the idea that God is disappointed is a powerful one that's hard to let go of. It takes a work of the Spirit to make a knowledge of God's pleasure part of your lived experience.

During the study, be thoughtful about whether there might be any space at all between what people know are the right Sunday-school answers and what they might feel in their gut. It may help to distinguish between the idea of *formal* theology, which is what you would normally say you believe, and *functional* theology. Functional theology is the old, under-the-skin heart-suspicion that may be in total contradiction with a person's formal theology, but when push comes to shove might be more powerful.

LESSON 5: THE SEARCH FOR WISDOM

People in the ancient world did not draw a sharp distinction between knowledge and wisdom. To them, an understanding of the natural world was connected to an understanding of ethics, or principles for human societies, or a knowledge of God. This means that in Job 28, for instance, an excursus about mining is not a poetic rabbit trail. Consideration of that realm informs the way we understand another subject (in this case, the pursuit of wisdom). Lesson 4 had a similar reflection, as the life cycle of trees informed thoughts about human mortality. The larger question is, *How does the world work?* And the endeavor of seeking answers is not merely academic or abstract. We understand how the world works so that we can live well within it, with humility and insight. If that is true about botany, or zoology, or meteorology, how much more about theology! The end of the chapter declares that the knowledge of God and a lived knowledge of ethics is the doorway to wisdom and understanding writ large.

Not all participants will be in the same place as they navigate these big questions about how the world works. Some may question the truth that Jesus holds all things together. But whatever our formal beliefs, we all have something in common. At times, we are all resistant to the idea that what we need at this moment is relational engagement with Jesus. Even we who are Sunday school graduates and church people from way back, who sign off on Christian doctrine and disciplines *in principle*, will *in practice* dig in our heels and avoid eye contact with Jesus. Sometimes our hearts recoil even from our kind Savior. In those times, we need to be rescued from our irrational reluctance to engage with Jesus.

EXERCISE: The summary of Job 28 is to fear the Lord and turn away from evil. The article doesn't address the need to turn away from evil, but the exercise invites your group to consider how that admonition fits into the bigger discovery of wisdom and the maintenance of a relationship with the God of wisdom. Hearing that turning from evil means loving other people may sound too easy—or maybe too hard! Our hearts are stingy, reluctant to give to others or be a friend. Perhaps we're attracted to a more intellectual, cognitive kind of wisdom. But the fuller passage from James 3 says, "Who is wise and understanding among you? By his good conduct let him show his works in the meekness of wisdom. But if you have bitter jealousy and selfish ambition in your hearts, do not boast and be false to the truth. This is not the wisdom that comes down from above, but is earthly, unspiritual, demonic. For where jealousy and selfish ambition exist, there will be disorder and every vile practice. But the wisdom from above is first pure, then peaceable, gentle, open to reason, full of mercy and good fruits, impartial and sincere" (vv. 13–17). In God's economy there is no wisdom that is primarily cognitive.

LESSON 6: LOSING EVERYTHING

The status Job once held in his community is significant. It wasn't just that he was young, good-looking, and rich. Chapter 29 details how Job was a generous man of integrity and character, who stood up for justice—the kind of person you and I might aspire to be. This gives extra fodder for thought as we meditate on Job's story alongside Jesus's story. Like Job, Jesus hadn't just not done anything wrong; Jesus actively went about doing good (Acts 10:38), and suffered for it. In this way, Job's life profoundly prefigures Jesus.

In fact, loss is a theme in many parts of the Bible. In the book of Lamentations, the prophet Jeremiah walks through the ruins of Jerusalem in disbelief and sorrow, and he says, "Look and see if there is any sorrow like my sorrow" (Lamentations 1:12). The composer George Frederick Handel, in his *Messiah*, takes that verse and inserts it into the story of the suffering of Christ: "Behold, and see if there be any sorrow like unto his sorrow." It's brilliant, the way Handel maps the story of Christ and his suffering onto the bigger story of Israel and of humanity.

So when someone asks, "Is there any sorrow like mine?" one answer is yes. Whether we ask the question ourselves in a moment of pain, or whether Job or Jeremiah asks it, none of us is alone in the experience. Although deep loss can feel profoundly lonely, like no one else can know how we feel, part of what the Bible gives us is the knowledge that it is a shared experience. But when we ask the question about Jesus, "Is there any sorrow like his?" the answer is also no. In this case it's not the type of suffering, but the degree of suffering. No one ever has suffered loss and deprivation to the degree that Jesus did. The consideration of the sorrow of Christ makes us shut our mouths as we offer our own lamentations. Though our sorrow is great, his is greater.

LESSON 7: THE PROBLEM OF INJUSTICE

The belief in a just universe is deeply rooted in the human psyche. We want it to be true that good things will come to people who do good. But our experience tells us that immediate and automatic "good karma" for good living is not characteristic of the world we live in.

Job is not a book of systematic theology. But it may be helpful to articulate a few broad biblical principles taught by the Scriptures as a whole.

All of God's creatures enjoy the benefits of "common grace." As Jesus says in the Sermon on the Mount, God "makes his sun rise on the evil and on the good, and sends rain on the just and the unjust" (Matthew 5:45). All of us daily enjoy benefits that we did nothing to bring about.

Suffering is an outworking of life in a broken world, but not necessarily the direct result of sinful choices. All of us suffer because of the fall; this world post-Eden has become characterized by disease and disability, storms and drought, frustration and death. But our individual specific sufferings may or may not be connected to any sin of our own.

God's world is built in such a way as to affirm the wisdom of living life according to his commands. In general, most of the time, living in God's world according to God's commands tends toward better outcomes. The Book of Proverbs teaches, do what's right and you will prosper. In general terms, that seems to be the way God has set his world up.

Suffering is sometimes the outcome of doing good. In a world in rebellion against God, often those who do good are resented and opposed. The Bible is full of examples of people who suffer as a result of their faithfulness to God; Jesus of course is the prime example. Following Jesus means loving people; loving people means taking their trouble on yourself.

In God's providence suffering can have good purposes that are unknown to us. God in his goodness can make suffering redemptive. It can be, in his hands, purposeful; he can use it to accomplish better things. But often at the time this is invisible to us.

Sometimes suffering is connected to the work of the devil. Satan is the thief who comes to steal, kill, and destroy. Like the landowner in Matthew 13:28, sometimes we survey trouble, misery, and brokenness and can only say, "An enemy did this" (NIV).

No one can stand on the basis of their own good life; we live—in this world and the next—by mercy. When we know ourselves accurately, we appeal not for justice but for mercy. Knowing that we live under the grace of God, we live lives of gratitude and not entitlement.

LESSON 8: WORDS FROM THE WHIRLWIND

Augustine wrote about the Old and New Testaments, "The New is in the Old concealed; the Old is in the New revealed."[3] Hopefully, this is what you've experienced in this study guide. The meaning of an Old Testament book like Job is unfolded in a richer, more life-giving way as we read it in light of the New Testament. We understand it better when we read it in the context of the full canon of Scripture.

Reading backwards, beautiful things about Jesus the coming Messiah fairly leap off the page in many places in the Old Testament. But reading forwards, what seems like it should've been apparent often wasn't! First Peter 1:10–12 gives us a flavor for it: even prophets who knew that they were speaking of the Messiah only glimpsed, in shadows, the richness of what they themselves prophesied. As they spoke about Christ, they "were serving not themselves" but us who would hear in plain terms about the one who came to save.

There was so much that Job didn't know. And of course there is much that we don't know, either! But the mystery of Christ as revealed in the New Testament is a powerful indicator that the things we do not know don't need to be feared. Our God has already turned out to be more good, more kind, and more gracious than anyone imagined. And we too, as we face so much that is perplexing to us in our circumstances and in our fallen world, may take the now-unfolded mystery of Christ as a strong reason to trust the Father when we don't understand what he is doing.

ENDNOTES

1. Woody Allen, dir., *Annie Hall* (Beverly Hills, CA: United Artists, 1977).

2. David Atkinson, *The Message of Job* (Downers Grove, IL: InterVarsity, 1991), 116.

3. Augustine, *Seven Questions about the Heptateuch* 2.73.